Pebble®
Plus

AMAZING SIGHTS OF THE SKY

Eclipses

by Martha E. H. Rustad

CAPSTONE PRESS
a capstone imprint

Pebble Plus is published by Capstone Press,
1710 Roe Crest Drive, North Mankato, Minnesota 56003
www.mycapstone.com

Library of Congress Cataloging-in-Publication Data
Library of Congress Cataloging-in-Publication data is available on the Library of Congress website.
ISBN 978-1-5157-6753-4 (library binding)
ISBN 978-1-5157-6759-6 (paperback)
ISBN 978-1-5157-6771-8 (eBook PDF)

Summary: Simple text introduces readers to solar and lunar eclipses, including why eclipses occur
and how often they occur.

Editorial Credits
Anna Butzer, editor; Juliette Peters, designer Wanda Winch, media researcher;
Steve Walker, production specialist

Photo Credits
Shutterstock: CHOATphotographer, 5, Chris Collins, 15, Igor Zh., cover, Jakinnboaz, 9, Joey
Santini, 13, muratart, 1, 11, 19, Nazar Yosyfiv, starfield background, sdecoret, 7, supot phanna, 21,
underworld, 17

Note to Parents and Teachers

The Amazing Sights of the Sky set supports national science standards related to earth science.
This book describes and illustrates eclipses. The images support early readers in understanding
the text. The repetition of words and phrases helps early readers learn new words. This book also
introduces early readers to subject-specific vocabulary words, which are defined in the Glossary
section. Early readers may need assistance to read some words and to use the Table of Contents,
Glossary, Read More, Internet Sites, Critical Thinking Questions, and Index sections of the book.

Printed and bound in the United States of America.
010695R

Table of Contents

What Is an Eclipse? 4

Solar Eclipse. 10

Lunar Eclipse. 14

See an Eclipse. 18

Glossary 22

Read More 23

Internet Sites 23

Critical Thinking Questions 24

Index 24

What Is an Eclipse?

An eclipse is like a game of hide-and-seek in space. The sun and moon take turns hiding from Earth.

The moon and Earth move in paths called orbits. Earth orbits the sun. The moon orbits Earth. Sometimes these paths line up. Then an eclipse happens.

We can see two kinds
of eclipses. The sun hides
during a solar eclipse.
The moon looks dark
in a lunar eclipse.

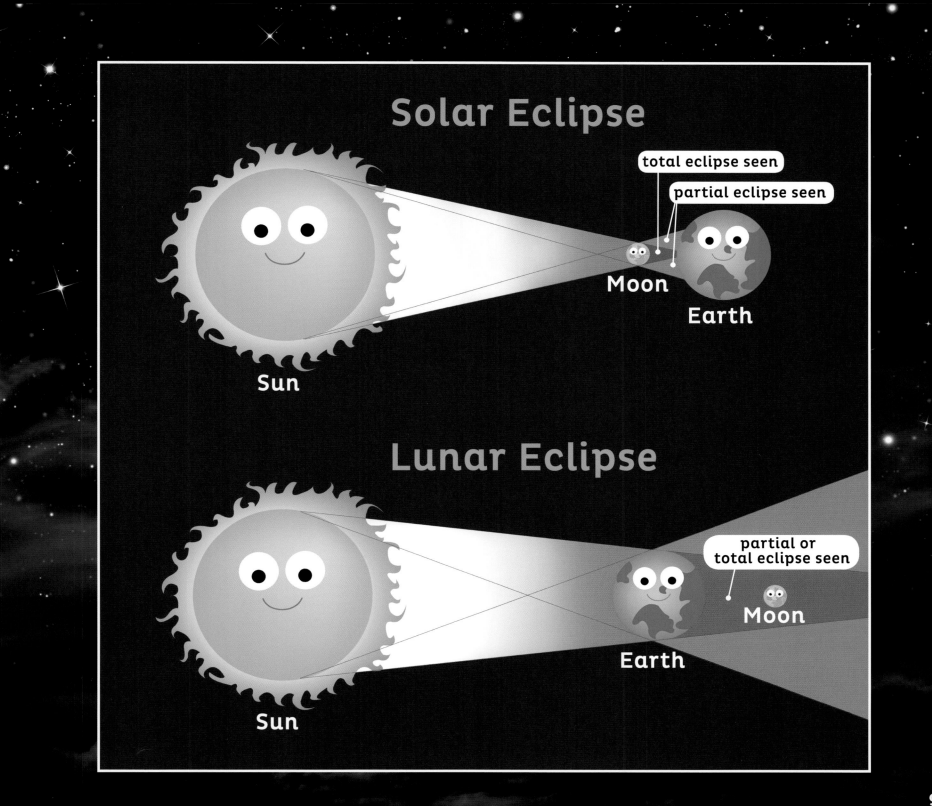

Solar Eclipse

The moon slowly moves in front of the sun in a solar eclipse. The sky grows dark. Sunlight makes a red glow behind the moon.

Eclipses cover either all or part of the sun. Total eclipses cover all of the sun. Partial eclipses cover part of the sun.

Lunar Eclipse

Sometimes, Earth passes

between the sun and moon.

A lunar eclipse happens.

Earth's shadow covers the moon.

The moon looks red or orange.

The moon needs sunlight to shine.

But Earth blocks the sunlight.

The moon goes dark

for about an hour.

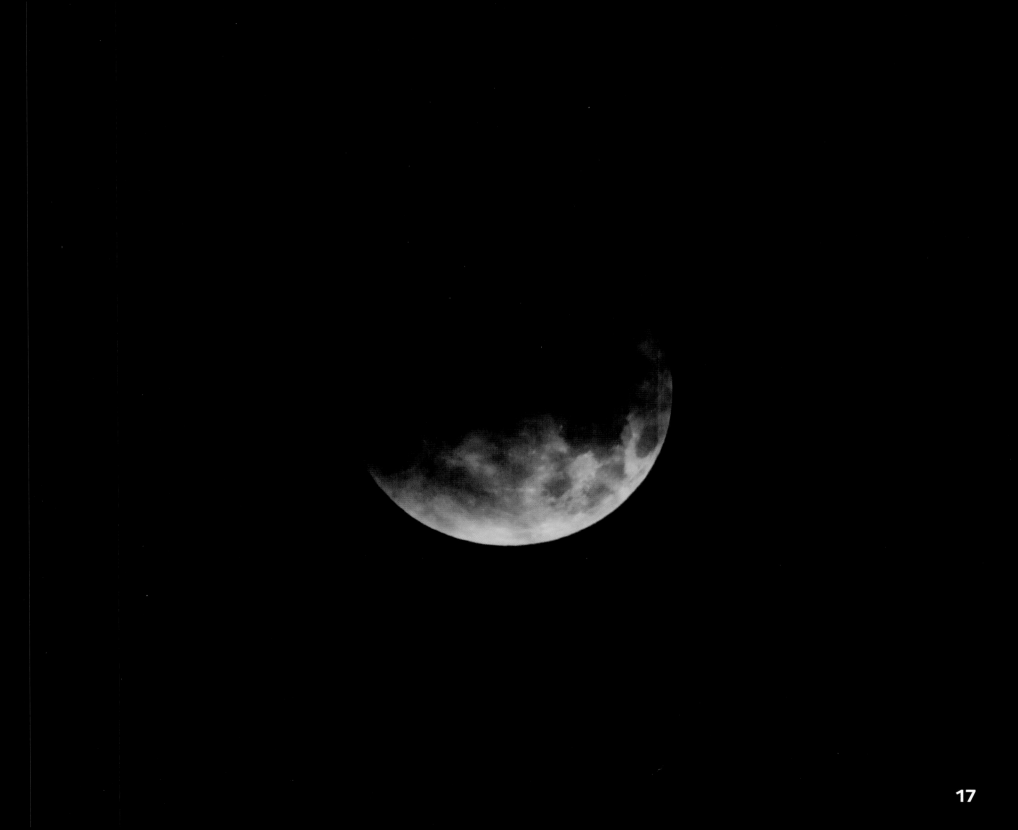

See an Eclipse

Up to three lunar eclipses happen each year. At least two partial solar eclipses happen each year. A total solar eclipse happens about every 18 months.

Scientists study earth and moon orbits.

They tell people when eclipses

will happen and where on Earth

you can see them.

You will see an amazing sight!

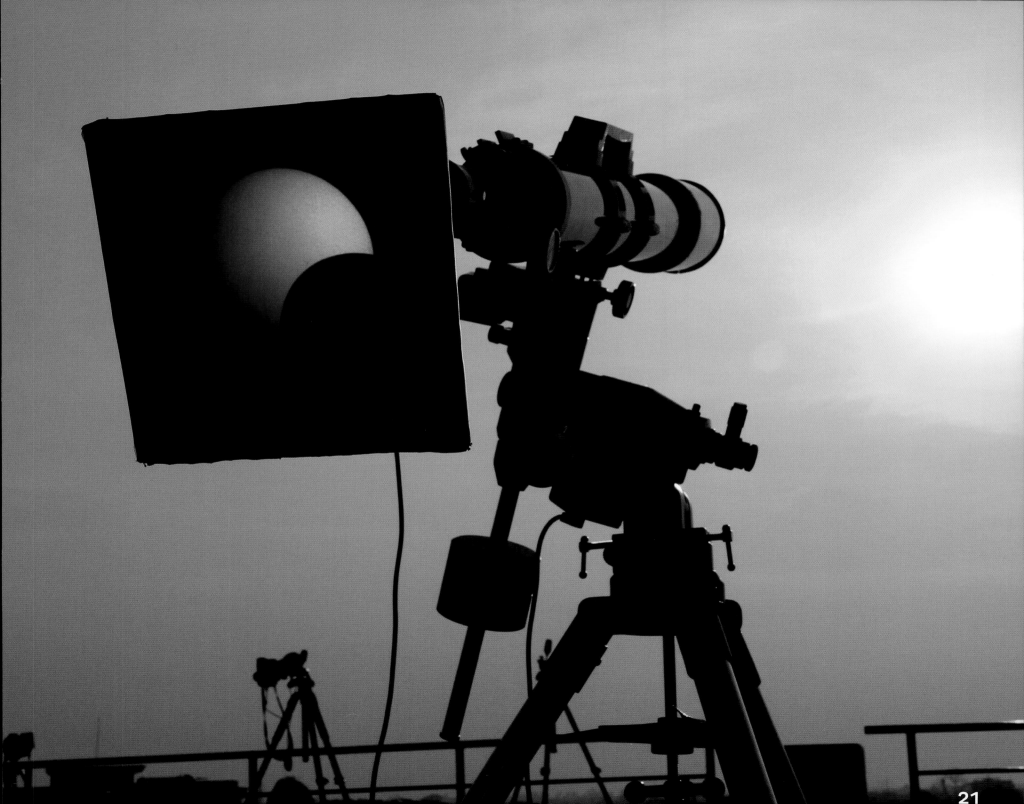

GLOSSARY

eclipse—to hide an object from view

lunar eclipse—when the Earth is directly between the sun and the moon; the Earth's shadow hides the moon from view; lunar eclipses happen only when the moon is full

moon—a large object that orbits a planet

orbit—a path that an object follows in space

solar eclipse—when the moon is between the sun and the Earth; the moon hides the sun from our view

sun—the large star at the center of our solar system

READ MORE

Hill, Carolyn L. *Journey Through Eclipses*. Spotlight on Space Science. New York: PowerKids Press, 2015.

Hunter, Nick. *Eclipses*. The Night Sky: And Other Amazing Sights in Space. Chicago: Heinemann, 2014.

Portman, Michael. *What Is an Eclipse?* Space Mysteries. New York: Gareth Stevens, 2014.

INTERNET SITES

Use FactHound to find Internet sites related to this book.

Visit *www.facthound.com*

Just type 9781515767534 and go.

Check out projects, games and lots more at
www.capstonekids.com

CRITICAL THINKING QUESTIONS

1. How does a solar eclipse happen?

2. How many lunar eclipses can happen each year?

3. Why do you think the moon looks red or orange during a lunar eclipse?

INDEX

Earth, 4, 6, 14,
  16, 20
moon, 4, 6, 8, 10,
  14, 16, 20
orbits, 6, 20
partial eclipses, 12, 18

scientists, 20
shadows, 14
sun, 4, 6, 8, 10, 12, 14
total eclipses, 12, 18